Dusk to Dawn

POEMS OF NIGHT

SELECTED BY
HELEN HILL, AGNES PERKINS,
AND ALETHEA HELBIG

ILLUSTRATED BY ANNE BURGESS

THOMAS Y. CROWELL / NEW YORK

Dusk to Dawn
Text copyright © 1981 by Helen Hill, Agnes Perkins, and Alethea Helbig
Illustrations copyright © 1981 by Anne Burgess
For information address Thomas Y. Crowell Junior Books, 10 East 53rd Street,
New York, N.Y. 10022. Published simultaneously in Canada by
Fitzhenry & Whiteside Limited, Toronto.
Designed by Al Cetta

Library of Congress Cataloging in Publication Data
Main entry under title:

Dusk to dawn.

  Includes indexes.
  SUMMARY: A collection of poems with nocturnal themes.
  1. Night—Juvenile poetry. 2. Children's poetry,
American. [1. Night—Poetry. 2. American and British poetry—Collections]
I. Hill, Helen, 1915–   II. Perkins, Agnes.
III. Helbig, Alethea. IV. Burgess, Anne, 1942–
PS595.N54D8   821'.008'033   80–770
ISBN 0–690–04065–2
ISBN 0–690–04066–0 (lib. bdg.)

1 2 3 4 5 6 7 8 9 10
First Edition

Acknowledgments

Acknowledgment is made for permission to reprint the following copyrighted material: "Andrew's Bedtime Story" and "Falling Asleep" from *Happily Ever After* by Ian Serraillier, published by Oxford University Press (1963). Copyright © 1963 by Ian Serraillier. Reprinted by permission of Ian Serraillier. "Aunt Sue's Stories" and "Winter Moon," copyright 1926 by Alfred A. Knopf and renewed 1954 by Langston Hughes. Reprinted from *Selected Poems of Langston Hughes* by Langston Hughes, by permission of Alfred A. Knopf, Inc. "The Bird of Night" and "The Mockingbird" reprinted with permission of Macmillan Publishing Co., Inc., and Penguin Books Ltd. from *The Bat-Poet* by Randall Jarrell. Copyright © Macmillan Publishing Co., Inc., 1963, 1964. "The Mockingbird" originally appeared in *The New Yorker*. "Child's Game" from *The Village and Other Poems* by Judson Jerome, published by Trunk Press, 1976. Reprinted by permission of Judson Jerome. "Cows Are Coming Home in Maine," reprinted with permission of Macmillan Publishing Co., Inc., from *Collected Poems* by Robert P. Tristram Coffin. Copyright 1938 by Macmillan Publishing Co., Inc., renewed 1966 by Margaret Coffin Halvosa. "The Dark" from *Poor Roy* by Roy Fuller. Reprinted by permission of Andre Deutsch Ltd. "Delicate the Toad," copyright © 1964 by Robert Francis, and "Night Train," copyright © 1936, 1964 by Robert Francis, reprinted from *Robert Francis: Collected Poems, 1936–1976* (University of Massachusetts Press, 1976). "Doll's Boy 's Asleep" is reprinted from *Tulips & Chimneys* by e. e. cummings, edited by George James Firmage. By permission of Liveright Publishing Corporation. Copyright 1923, 1925 and renewed 1951, 1953 by e. e. cummings. Copyright © 1973, 1976 by Nancy T. Andrews. Copyright © 1973, 1976 by George James Firmage. Published in Great Britain in *The Complete Poems 1913–1962* by e. e. cummings. By permission of Granada Publishing Ltd. "Down Dip the Branches" and "Dunce Song 6" from *Collected and New Poems 1924–1963* by Mark Van Doren. Copyright © 1963 by Mark Van Doren. Reprinted with the permission of Hill and Wang (now a division of Farrar, Straus and Giroux, Inc.). "Early Supper" from *Light and Dark* by Barbara Howes. Copyright © 1959 by Barbara Howes. Reprinted by permission of Wesleyan University Press. "Early Supper" first appeared in *The New Yorker*. "A Gaggle of Geese, a Pride

Contents

Dusk to Dawn

Where the Hayfields Were

Coming down the mountain in the twilight—
April it was and quiet in the air—
I saw an old man and his little daughter
Burning the meadows where the hayfields were.

Forksful of flame he scattered in the meadows.
Sparkles of fire in the quiet air
Burned in their circles and the silver flowers
Danced like candles where the hayfields were,—

Danced as she did in enchanted circles,
Curtseyed and danced along the quiet air:
Slightly she danced in the stillness, in the twilight,
Dancing in the meadows where the hayfields were.

ARCHIBALD MacLEISH

Cows Are Coming Home in Maine

Cows are coming home in Maine
Through juniper and bayberry,
And half the world is lacy fir,
And half the world is sea.

Along the stonewalls and the dusk
The cow-paths come up very steep,
The cow-bells mingle with the bells
That ring on reefs out on the deep.

It is growing dark, and stars
And lighthouse lamps burn through the blue,
But the ferns still show up green
With the afterglow and dew.

The cows come swinging, nose to tail,
With day's light on their western sides,
Clean and homely from the fields
Sloping to mystery and the tides.

Their mouths are full of wild, sweet things,
But they move their fragrant cud
Side to side, as if they had
Nothing but comfort in their blood.

Under the night-hawks, high and strange,
Through beauty which is almost pain,
Through wild juniper by the sea,
The cows are coming home in Maine.

Robert P. Tristram Coffin

Down Dip the Branches

Down dip the branches,
The long leafy branches,
Down dip the branches
To bring old robin in.

Underneath the haytops,
The warm windy haytops,
Underneath the haytops
The mice are creeping home.

Soon it will be sunset,
Red and yellow sunset,
Soon it will be sunset,
With everything indoors.

Apples for supper.
Sing, sing for supper.
After, after supper,
Sing awhile in bed.

Mouse in the meadow,
The green sleepy meadow,
Mouse in the meadow,
Fold your little paws.

Robin in the branches,
The dark sleepy branches,
Old robin in the branches,
Shut, shut, shut your eyes.

MARK VAN DOREN

4

Delicate the Toad

Delicate the toad
Sits and sips
The evening air.

He is satisfied
With dust, with
Color of dust.

A hopping shadow
Now, and now
A shadow still.

Laugh, you birds
At one so
Far from flying

But have you
Caught, among small
Stars, his flute?

ROBERT FRANCIS

The Toadstool Wood

The toadstool wood is dark and mouldy,
  And has a ferny smell.
About the trees hangs something quiet
  And queer—like a spell.

Beneath the arching sprays of bramble
  Small creatures make their holes;
Over the moss's close green velvet
  The stilted spider strolls.

The stalks of toadstools pale and slender
  That grow from that old log,
Bars they might be to imprison
  A prince turned to a frog.

There lives no mumbling witch nor wizard
  In this uncanny place,
Yet you might think you saw at twilight
  A little, crafty face.

JAMES REEVES

6

The Park at Evening

I like the park best at evening, on a cool day,
When the children's voices sound thin and sweet,
Hanging in the air like shreds of clouds.
And birches at the edge of the park grow frail,
Grow misty like a line of smoke, low and small
At the very edge of our eyesight,
At the edge of the park.

I like it when hiding children
Come running from behind trees and bushes.
"All in, all in," they call.
Just as the parkkeeper rings his bell,
Sending them home, where their mothers
In lit kitchens are cooking sausages,
Growing the smallest bit anxious,
As the park turns gently into evening.

LESLIE NORRIS

The Mockingbird

Look one way and the sun is going down,
Look the other and the moon is rising.
The sparrow's shadow's longer than the lawn.
The bats squeak: "Night is here," the birds cheep:
    "Day is gone."
On the willow's highest branch, monopolizing
Day and night, cheeping, squeaking, soaring,
The mockingbird is imitating life.

All day the mockingbird has owned the yard.
As light first woke the world, the sparrows trooped
Onto the seedy lawn: the mockingbird
Chased them off shrieking. Hour by hour, fighting hard
To make the world his own, he swooped
On thrushes, thrashers, jays, and chickadees—
At noon he drove away a big black cat.

Now, in the moonlight, he sits here and sings.
A thrush is singing, then a thrasher, then a jay—
Then, all at once, a cat begins meowing.
A mockingbird can sound like anything.
He imitates the world he drove away
So well that for a minute, in the moonlight,
Which one's the mockingbird? which one's the world?

RANDALL JARRELL

Early Supper

Laughter of children brings
    The kitchen down with laughter.
While the old kettle sings
Laughter of children brings
To a boil all savory things.
    Higher than beam or rafter,
Laughter of children brings
    The kitchen down with laughter.

So ends an autumn day,
    Light ripples on the ceiling,
Dishes are stacked away;
So ends an autumn day,
The children jog and sway
    In comic dances wheeling.
So ends an autumn day,
    Light ripples on the ceiling.

They trail upstairs to bed,
    And night is a dark tower.
The kettle calls: instead
They trail upstairs to bed,
Leaving warmth, the coppery-red
    Mood of their carnival hour.
They trail upstairs to bed,
    And night is a dark tower.

BARBARA HOWES

A Pavane for the Nursery

Now touch the air softly,
Step gently. One, two . . .
I'll love you till roses
Are robin's-egg blue;
I'll love you till gravel
Is eaten for bread,
And lemons are orange,
And lavender's red.

Now touch the air softly,
Swing gently the broom.
I'll love you till windows
Are all of a room;
And the table is laid,
And the table is bare,
And the ceiling reposes
On bottomless air.

I'll love you till Heaven
Rips the stars from his coat,
And the Moon rows away in

A glass-bottomed boat;
And Orion steps down
Like a diver below,
And Earth is ablaze,
And Ocean aglow.

So touch the air softly,
And swing the broom high.
We will dust the gray mountains,
And sweep the blue sky;
And I'll love you as long
As the furrow the plow,
As However is Ever,
And Ever is Now.

WILLIAM JAY SMITH

Dunce Song 6

Her hand in my hand,
Soft as the south wind,
Soft as a colt's nose,
Soft as forgetting;

Her cheek to my cheek,
Red as the cranberry,
Red as a mitten,
Red as remembering—

Here we go round like raindrops,
Raindrops,
Here we go round
So snug together,

Oh, but I wonder,
Oh, but I know,
Who comforts like raisins,
Who kisses like snow.

MARK VAN DOREN

Child's Game
(for J. Y., 1954–1957)

tick-a-lock rock-a-bye
chopper-chin peeper-eye
Janey with a crooked smile
switched her pony-tail and blew
all three candles peek-a-boo
toddled all her crooked mile
upsy-daisy ring-around
ashes ashes we all fall down
    night night sleep tight

we all fall down hold hands around
hands are home fingers steeple
open the door blackbirds soar
all the while a crooked file
of moon rain and memory Jane
hide-and-seek in hearts of people
see the pretty petals close
dreaming comes gaming goes
    night night sleep tight

JUDSON JEROME

14

Aunt Sue's Stories

Aunt Sue has a head full of stories.
Aunt Sue has a whole heart full of stories.
Summer nights on the front porch
Aunt Sue cuddles a brown-faced child to her bosom
And tells him stories.

Black slaves
Working in the hot sun,
And black slaves
Walking in the dewy night,
And black slaves
Singing sorrow songs on the banks of a mighty river
Mingle themselves softly
In the flow of old Aunt Sue's voice,
Mingle themselves softly
In the dark shadows that cross and recross
Aunt Sue's stories.

And the dark-faced child, listening,
Knows that Aunt Sue's stories are real stories.
He knows that Aunt Sue never got her stories
Out of any book at all,
But that they came
Right out of her own life.

The dark-faced child is quiet
Of a summer night
Listening to Aunt Sue's stories.

LANGSTON HUGHES

Andrew's Bedtime Story

I told him a tale that I adore
Called *Theseus and the Minotaur,*
Of how a prince with a ball of wool
   That his girl friend Ariadne gave him,
Was forced to search for a fiery bull
   Through cave and labyrinth. Keen to save him,
She said, "Unwind the wool as you go
Through the twisting corridors down below,
And return to me safe—I love you so."

That was the start of the tale I told,
And Andrew listened, as good as gold.
Next day when he ran home from school,
He found a skein of his mother's wool,
Unwound it, tied it to door and chair,
Along the passage and up the stair,
     Yes, everywhere.
  I opened the door of my room
     To find
Pitschi the cat with his legs entwined,
Jane and Helen flat on the floor,

Great-aunt almost sliced at the knees
(As wire at the grocer's slices cheese),
    All of them trapped.
    The thread I snapped,
With scissors and knife I hacked away
    And set them free.
    But where was A?
There, in a corner lurking, laughing.
    "No more
  Of Ariadne's thread,

My boy," I cried, "or we'll all be dead!"
I stalked away.

But a murderous thread not seen before
Tripped me up, and I cracked my head.

IAN SERRAILLIER

The Happy Family

Before the children say goodnight,
    Mother, Father, stop and think:
Have you screwed their heads on tight?
    Have you washed their ears with ink?

Have you said and done and thought
    All that earnest parents should?
Have you beat them as you ought?
    Have you begged them to be good?

And above all—when you start
    Out the door and douse the light—
Think, be certain, search your heart:
    Have you screwed their heads on tight?

If they sneeze when they're asleep,
    Will their little heads come off?
If they just breathe very deep?
    If—especially—they cough?

Should—alas!—the little dears
    Lose a little head or two,
Have you inked their little ears:
    Girls' ears pink and boys' ears blue?

Children's heads are very loose.
    Mother, Father, screw them tight.
If you feel uncertain use
    A monkey wrench, but do it right.

If a head should come unscrewed
    You will know that you have failed.

19

Doubtful cases should be glued.
  Stubborn cases should be nailed.

Then when all your darlings go
  Sweetly screaming off to bed,
Mother, Father, you may know
  Angels guard each little head.

Come the morning you will find
  One by one each little head
Full of gentle thoughts and kind,
  Sweetly screaming to be fed.

JOHN CIARDI

Falling Asleep

I can't fall asleep
When Mummy goes to choir. I've said
My prayers, the cat is purring on my bed,
And Daddy's reading downstairs. My head
   Lies pillowed deep,
   But I can't fall asleep,

   I can't fall asleep
Or settle. Though Mummy has undressed me
And bathed me and bedded me and kissed me,
I wonder—while she's singing—has she missed me?
   Will I never fall asleep?
   The long hours creep,

   The long hours creep
So slowly . . . Then at last the front door
Bangs, and I hear her cross the floor.
I call good night and she kisses me once more
   And hugs me. I could weep
   For joy. But I fall asleep.

IAN SERRAILLIER

Doll's Boy 's Asleep

Doll's boy 's asleep
under a stile
he sees eight and twenty
ladies in a line

the first lady
says to nine ladies
his lips drink water
but his heart drinks wine

the tenth lady
says to nine ladies
they must chain his foot
for his wrist 's too fine

the nineteenth
says to nine ladies
you take his mouth
for his eyes are mine.

Doll's boy 's asleep
under the stile
for every mile the feet go
the heart goes nine

e. e. cummings

Lullaby

The long canoe
Toward the shadowy shore,
One . . . two . . .
Three . . . four . . .
The paddle dips,
Turns in the wake,
Pauses, then
Forward again.
Water drips
From the blade to the lake.
Nothing but that,
No sound of wings;
The owl and bat
Are velvet things.
No wind awakes,
No fishes leap;
No rabbits creep
Among the brakes.
The long canoe

At the shadowy shore,
One . . . two . . .
Three . . . four . . .
A murmur now
Under the prow
Where rushes bow
To let us through.
One . . . two . . .
Upon the shore,
Three . . . four . . .
Upon the lake,
No one's awake,
No one's awake,
One . . . two . . .
No one, not even you.

ROBERT HILLYER

John's Song

It's a long walk in the dark
on the blind side of the moon
and it's a long day without water
when the river's gone
and it's hard listening to no voice
when you're all alone

so take a hundred lighted candles with you
when you walk on the moon
and quickly quickly tie a knot in the river
before the water's gone
and listen for my voice, if for no other
when you're all alone

JOAN AIKEN

The Dark

I feared the darkness as a boy;
And if at night I had to go
Upstairs alone I'd make a show
Of carrying on with those below
A dialogue of shouts and "whats?"
So they'd be sure to save poor Roy
Were he attacked by vampire bats.

Or thugs or ghosts. But far less crude
Than criminal or even ghost
Behind a curtain or a post
Was what I used to dread the most—
The always-unseen bugaboo
Of black-surrounded solitude.
I dread it still at sixty-two.

ROY FULLER

Rhyme for Night

Dark is soft, like fur
Velvet, like a purr;
Lies warm, lies close
On fingers and toes

If dark cost much money
Rich men only
Would be able to pay
And rest them from day

If dark were not given
Each night from heaven
On field and town and park
Men would have to make dark

Dark is so warm, so deep
Without dark, how could we sleep?

JOAN AIKEN

The Open Door

Out of the dark
to the sill of the door
lay the snow in a long
unruffled floor,
and the lamplight fell
narrow and thin
a carpet unrolled
for the cat to walk in.
Slowly, smoothly,
black as the night,
with paws unseen
(white upon white)
like a queen who walks
down a corridor
the black cat paced
that cold smooth floor,
and left behind her,
bead upon bead,
the track of small feet
like dark fern seed.

ELIZABETH COATSWORTH

A Gaggle of Geese, a Pride of Lions

These are the nights when the geese
talk their way north,
taking it low in the scant clouds
over my house. The town lights
bother them and they wheel back
upon themselves to find a turn
of power to make the dash,
loud and clear and gone away north.

My cat hears them and paces the rug,
each step sinking to the joint
in the nap as if it were some hot sand
where her mate waited and watched
and the cubs tangled like liquid buckskin
across the sofa back.

JOHN MOORE

The Woods at Night

The binocular owl,
fastened to a limb
like a lantern
all night long,

sees where all
the other birds sleep:
towhee under leaves,
titmouse deep

in a twighouse,
sapsucker gripped
to a knothole lip,
redwing in the reeds,

swallow in the willow,
flicker in the oak—

but cannot see poor
whippoorwill

under the hill
in deadbrush nest,
who's awake, too—
with stricken eye

flayed by the moon
her brindled breast
repeats, repeats, repeats its plea
for cruelty.

MAY SWENSON

The Bird of Night

A shadow is floating through the moonlight.
Its wings don't make a sound.
Its claws are long, its beak is bright.
Its eyes try all the corners of the night.

It calls and calls: all the air swells and heaves
And washes up and down like water.
The ear that listens to the owl believes
In death. The bat beneath the eaves,

The mouse beside the stone are still as death—
The owl's air washes them like water.
The owl goes back and forth inside the night,
And the night holds its breath.

RANDALL JARRELL

Nocturn Cabbage

Cabbages catch at the moon.
It is late summer, no rain, the pack of the soil
    cracks open, it is a hard summer.
In the night the cabbages catch at the moon, the
    leaves drip silver, the rows of cabbages are
    series of little silver waterfalls in the moon.

CARL SANDBURG

Winter Moon

How thin and sharp is the moon tonight!
How thin and sharp and ghostly white
Is the slim curved crook of the moon tonight!

LANGSTON HUGHES

Night Train

Across the dim frozen fields of night
Where is it going, where is it going?
No throb of wheels, no rush of light.
Only a whistle blowing, blowing.
Only a whistle blowing.

Something echoing through my brain,
Something timed between sleep and waking,
Murmurs, murmurs this may be the train
I must be sometime, somewhere taking,
I must be sometime taking.

ROBERT FRANCIS

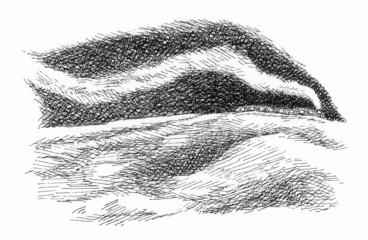

Night Landscape

Rolling and tossing out sparkles like roses
puffing out plum-coloured smoke as it goes is
a cedarwood train
on an ebony plain
whose passenger muses or gazes or dozes

the boy on the train is guard, passenger, driver
who reads while he drives, while the train, like a diver,
soars, plunges, and swoops
describes hundreds of loops
all veiled in its vapour like Lady Godiva

the boy is the track is the train is the cedar
from which it was carved, is the book, is the reader
who turns out the light
and shoots into night
and spends all his dream playing follow-my-leader

JOAN AIKEN

36

Giant Thunder

Giant Thunder, striding home,
Wonders if his supper's done.

"Hag wife, hag wife, bring me my bones!"
"They are not done," the old hag moans.

"Not done? not done?" the giant roars
And heaves his old wife out of doors.

Cries he, "I'll have them, cooked or not!"
But overturns the cooking-pot.

He flings the burning coals about;
See how the lightning flashes out!

Upon the gale the old hag rides,
The cloudy moon for terror hides.

All the world with thunder quakes;
Forest shudders, mountain shakes;
From the cloud the rainstorm breaks;
Village ponds are turned to lakes;
Every living creature wakes.

Hungry Giant, lie you still!
Stamp no more from hill to hill—
Tomorrow you shall have your fill.

JAMES REEVES

The Ride-By-Nights

Up on their brooms the Witches stream,
Crooked and black in the crescent's gleam;
One foot high, and one foot low,
Bearded, cloaked, and cowled, they go.
'Neath Charlie's Wane they twitter and tweet,
And away they swarm 'neath the Dragon's feet,
With a whoop and a flutter they swing and sway,
And surge pell-mell down the Milky Way.
Between the legs of the glittering Chair
They hover and squeak in the empty air.
Then round they swoop past the glimmering Lion
To where Sirius barks behind huge Orion;
Up, then, and over to wheel amain
Under the silver, and home again.

WALTER DE LA MARE

The Magic Wood

The wood is full of shining eyes,
The wood is full of creeping feet,
The wood is full of tiny cries:
You must not go to the wood at night!

I met a man with eyes of glass
And a finger as curled as the wriggling worm,
And hair all red with rotting leaves,
And a stick that hissed like a summer snake.

He sang me a song in backwards words,
And drew me a dragon in the air.
I saw his teeth through the back of his head,
And a rat's eyes winking from his hair.

He made me a penny out of a stone,
And showed me the way to catch a lark
With a straw and a nut and a whispered word
And a pennorth of ginger wrapped up in a leaf.

He asked me my name, and where I lived;
I told him a name from my Book of Tales;
He asked me to come with him into the wood
And dance with the Kings from under the hills.

But I saw that his eyes were turning to fire;
I watched the nails grow on his wriggling hand;
And I said my prayers, all out in a rush,
And found myself safe on my father's land.

Oh, the wood is full of shining eyes,
The wood is full of creeping feet,
The wood is full of tiny cries:
You must not go to the wood at night!

HENRY TREECE

What Did I Dream?

What did I dream? I do not know—
  The fragments fly like chaff.
Yet, strange, my mind was tickled so
  I cannot help but laugh.

Pull the curtains close again,
  Tuck me grandly in;
Must a world of humour wane
  Because birds begin

Complaining in a fretful tone,
  Rousing me from sleep—
The finest entertainment known,
  And given rag-cheap?

ROBERT GRAVES

The Horses

It has turned to snow in the night.
The horses have put on
their long fur stockings
and they are wearing
fur capes with high necks
out of which the device
of their ears makes four statues.
Their tales have caught flecks
of snow and hang down
loose as bedsheets.
They stand nose to nose
in the blue light that coats
the field before sunup
and rub dry their old kisses.

MAXINE KUMIN

43

The Huntsmen

Three jolly gentlemen,
In coats of red,
Rode their horses
Up to bed.

Three jolly gentlemen
Snored till morn,
Their horses champing
The golden corn.

Three jolly gentlemen,
At break of day,
Came clitter-clatter down the stairs
And galloped away.

WALTER DE LA MARE

Good Morning

Good morning to the great trees
That bend above this little house;
Good morning to the wind that comes
And goes among the leaves, and sings;
Good morning to the birds, the grass,
Good morning to the bare ground;
Good morning, pond across the way
That must have opened both its eyes;
Good morning, everything that shines
Or doesn't shine; good morning, mole
And worm and nesting mouse—good morning,
Morning to all things that ever
Were and will be, and that are.

MARK VAN DOREN

Index of Poets

Index of First Lines

Index of Titles

HELEN HILL, AGNES PERKINS, AND ALETHEA HELBIG have long been concerned as parents and as teachers of children's literature that children read and hear poems of high quality. Here they have made available for children, and for the adults who will share the book with them, a selection of modern poems that express the serenity and the mystery of night. The anthologists of *Dusk to Dawn* have been colleagues at Eastern Michigan University for more than fifteen years. They have collaborated on two other anthologies of contemporary verse, *Straight On Till Morning: Poems of the Imaginary World* and *New Coasts and Strange Harbors: Discovering Poems.*

ANNE BURGESS has illustrated several books for young readers, most recently *The Devil Take You, Barnabas Beane!,* and has had many of her line drawings published in *The New Yorker.* She and her husband, Perry Ashley, a stonemason, live on a farm near Boone, North Carolina.